The 1798 Rebellion

Photographs and memorabilia from the National Museum of Ireland

Michael Kenny

Country House, Dublin
in association with
The National Museum of Ireland

Published in 1996 by
Town House and Country House
Trinity House
Charleston Road
Ranelagh, Dublin 6
Ireland

in association with The National Museum of Ireland

Text copyright © The National Museum of Ireland, 1996

British Library Cataloguing in Publication Data. A catalogue record for this book is available from the British Library.

ISBN 0–946172–50–1

Acknowledgements
The author and publishers would like to thank the National Library for permission to reproduce Plates 13, 15 and 17.

Special thanks to Valerie Dowling and Brendan Doyle for photography, to Joseph Aylward, Karen Barker, Mary Barry, Teresa Breathnach and Deborah Ryan for their help and assistance and to Oliver Snoddy for his advice.

The kind assistance of the Ancient Order of Hibernians in the United States is also gratefully acknowledged.

Typesetting: Red Barn Publishing, Skibbereen
Printed in Ireland by ßetaprint

CONTENTS

THE BACKGROUND

The factors which combined to bring about the events of 1798 were many and varied. They included religious discrimination, the influence of American and French republicanism, a fast-growing population and endemic agrarian unrest. The Irish parliament in the 1790s was exclusively Protestant, despite the fact that Catholics formed the great majority of the population. Many other anti-Catholic laws had gradually and grudgingly been removed by legislation in 1778, 1782 and 1793, particularly restrictions on their right to inherit and purchase land, enter university, practise law and hold public office. Political and economic power remained firmly in the hands of Protestants, however, and they controlled the army, finance, education and the trade guilds. The confiscations of the seventeenth century and a comprehensive penal code for much of the eighteenth also ensured that they held a firm grip on the landed wealth of the country. Indeed, it has been estimated that, by the end of the 1770s, Catholics held a mere 5% of the land of Ireland.

Between 1767 and 1800, the population almost doubled, from 2.5 million to just under 5 million. A growth facilitated by the sub-division of farms, it had a profound effect on rural society. Increased competition for land caused agrarian violence and the spread of secret societies, such as Whiteboys, Oakboys and Peep o' Day Boys. In Ulster, this took on a sectarian form and culminated in the expulsion of several thousand Catholics from Armagh in 1795, following the formation of the Orange Order. The authorities did not intervene. Economic growth, especially the expansion of Belfast, Dublin and other urban centres, gave the impression that the country was improving. In some ways it was, but much of rural Ireland was in a state of 'smothered war', awaiting only a spark to ignite it.

The single most important outside influence on Irish affairs in the late eighteenth century was the American War of Independence. In the

late 1770s, the 'patriot' element in the Irish parliament, influenced by
the success of the Americans, began to press for legislative independence
from Britain and an end to trade restrictions on Irish goods. They were
supported by a large Volunteer force that had, ironically, been raised
to defend the country against America's ally, France.

*Photo 1.
Volunteer medals
c. 1779–80.
Volunteer units
sprang up all over
Ireland as the
American War of
Independence
drained the
country of regular
troops. The
movement became
a powerful
political force in
the agitation for
legislative
independence.*

In 1782 Britain accepted their demands and from this point the Irish
parliament was technically independent of Westminster, under the
Crown. Independence was more apparent than real, however. The Irish
executive, headed by the Viceroy, was appointed from London and
maintained control of affairs through patronage and appointments. The
country continued to be governed by what one modern historian has
described as a 'grotesque colonial partnership: a weak British Viceroy
with British staff, bullied by a narrow oligarchy of Irish Protestants of
British settler stock'. The concessions to the Irish parliament, which in
reality represented a small and corrupt oligarchy, only served to highlight
the grievances of those excluded from it. As the historian Thomas
Pakenham put it, the aims of the Volunteers 'had little more to do with

the mass of the Irish people than George Washington's with the Red Indians'. It is rather ironic, therefore, that later generations of nationalists were to look back upon 'Grattan's Parliament' as a golden age of freedom. Some leading figures, such as Henry Grattan himself, were political liberals, but they were in a minority. Indeed, the Irish parliament had few redeeming features other than its symbolic value and geographical location.

Photo 2. Henry Grattan (1746–1820). Leader of the campaign for Irish free trade in the late 1770s and for the independence of the Irish parliament in the early 1780s, Grattan was a brilliant orator and a charismatic figure. He opposed the Act of Union and campaigned for Catholic emancipation until his death in 1820.

The outbreak of the French Revolution in 1789 added a new and explosive element to an already unstable situation. As French ideas and armies spread across Europe, Irish radicals, despairing of reforming a thoroughly corrupt establishment, began to look towards France for deliverance.

THE SOCIETY OF UNITED IRISHMEN

The Society of United Irishmen was founded in Belfast in October 1791. The young radicals who set up the organisation, such as Wolfe Tone, Hamilton Rowan, Samuel Neilson and Thomas Russell, were much influenced by the momentous events taking place in Europe, but the movement contained people of various political shades, from cautious reformers to republican radicals. Their objective was 'an equal representation of all the people in parliament' and a political system which would include people of all religious persuasions. The demand for a separate republic came later.

Photos 3 a & b. Medal awarded 'for merit' by Napper Tandy, Captain of the Liberty Volunteers, 1782. Many of the United Irishmen, like Tandy, got their first taste of politics—and military activity—in the Volunteer movement.

The American struggle for independence had been greeted with particular enthusiasm in Ulster, where there was a strong and independent-minded Presbyterian community. Relatively prosperous and politically conscious, they occupied a middle ground, socially and economically, between the Protestant establishment and the Catholic majority. Having welcomed American independence, they now began to demand not only the removal of restrictions affecting themselves but also removal of the remaining laws against Catholics. The possibility of an alliance between the two groups was a cause for much alarm to the government.

As the shock waves of the French Revolution washed across Europe, William Pitt, the British Prime Minister, pressured the Irish parliament into repealing many of the remaining penal laws against Catholics. Relief Acts in 1792 and 1793 removed most of the disabilities but still barred Catholics from sitting in parliament or holding important offices of State. The hope was that concessions would ensure their loyalty in the face of the French threat. As in the case of earlier measures during the American War of Independence, the legislation was passed, not in a spirit of enlightenment as has sometimes been suggested, but rather in an attempt to secure the allegiance of a growing Catholic middle class.

Initially, the United Irish movement spread slowly outside of Ulster, except in Dublin where the veteran radical, Napper Tandy, became one of its leading figures. Many Catholics, after a century of discrimination, were slow to risk gains already made and their few

Photo 6. Samuel Neilson (1761–1803). A native of Co Down and founder member of the United Irishmen, he was arrested for sedition in 1796. Released in 1798, he was captured again during an attempt to free Lord Edward FitzGerald. Held at Fort George in Scotland until 1802, he was deported to Holland. He settled in America, where he died in 1803.

remaining gentry were as opposed to 'French principles' as were their Protestant equivalents.

THE ROAD TO REBELLION

Photo 7. Thomas Russell (1757–1803). A native of Cork and founder-member of the United Irishmen, he was arrested in 1798 and released in 1802. Went to Paris and met Robert Emmet, whom he assisted in his ill-fated rebellion. Arrested in Dublin, he was hanged on 21 October in Downpatrick, Co Down. Remembered as 'The Man from God Knows Where', from the title of a well-known poem.

In 1793 Britain went to war with France. Increasingly nervous of any manifestation of radicalism, the government suppressed the Volunteers. In 1794 the United Irishmen suffered the same fate. Several of its leaders, including Samuel Neilson, Thomas Russell, Henry Joy McCracken and Thomas Addis Emmet, came together and, in 1795, reconstituted the society as a secret, oath-bound body. In June of that year, Wolfe Tone left for America with the task of contacting the French and enlisting their aid for a rebellion in Ireland. At home the society began to develop a military structure and arm for war. Contact was made with agrarian societies such as the Defenders and some of the latter's grievances were taken on board, such as taxes, tithes and the price of land.

In 1796 Wolfe Tone sailed from America to France, where he convinced the ruling Directory to undertake an invasion of Ireland. In December of that year a French fleet, carrying fourteen thousand men,

set sail, under the veteran General Hoche. With them travelled Wolfe Tone, whose efforts, aided by Napper Tandy and Edward Lewins, had brought about the expedition. Unfortunately for the venture, General Hoche became separated from the main body and, as the fleet waited in Bantry Bay, it was dispersed by a storm. The survivors, including a bitterly disappointed Tone, struggled back to France.

Despite the set-back, the United Irishmen continued to plan for rebellion and in 1797 the government reacted with a 'scorched earth' policy, especially in the midlands and north. This put great pressure on the United Irish leaders and terrified their followers. In the meantime the liberal Viceroy Lord Fitzwilliam, who had been in favour of Catholic emancipation, was replaced by Lord Camden, who surrounded himself with advisers such as Lord Clare, John Beresford and John Foster, members of the very oligarchy whose attitudes and actions were responsible to a large degree for the dangerous state of the country. Raids for arms increased in frequency, assassinations of magistrates became

*Photos 9 a & b.
Medal awarded to
the Wicklow
Militia for the
suppression of
rebellion in County
Westmeath, 1797.*

*Photo 10. General
Lazare Hoche,
leader of the
unsuccessful Bantry
expedition, 1796.
His death the
following year was
a big blow to the
United Irishmen,
as he had been
committed to an
invasion of Ireland.*

commonplace and in parts of the country the aristocracy and gentry were in a state of panic. Reports that Napoleon was gathering an invasion fleet at Dunkirk added to the tension.

It was not in disturbed counties like Tipperary that the United Irishmen were strongest, however, but in 'quiet counties' like Kildare, where organisation was proceeding rapidly. A network of spies kept the government supplied with information, sometimes accurate, sometimes wildly exaggerated. By now, Dublin rather than Belfast was the headquarters of the revolutionary movement, whose leadership included several influential figures. Chief among these were Thomas Addis Emmet, son of the official state physician, William McNevin and John Lawless — both doctors — Arthur O'Connor, a radical aristocrat, Lord Edward FitzGerald, brother of the Duke of Leinster, and Oliver Bond, a rich wool merchant. The organisation had by now infiltrated into some of the most influential sections of Irish society. Lord Edward, who had some military experience, was the most charismatic of the group and also the most hot-headed.

Photo 11. William Corbet (1779–1842). An enthusiastic United Irishman, he was expelled from Trinity College in 1798 and joined the French army. Arrested later in Hamburg, he was brought back and lodged in Kilmainham jail. He escaped in 1803, rejoined the French army and had an illustrious military career.

Photo 12. Napoleon Bonaparte (1769–1821).

Photo 13. Arthur O'Connor (1763–1852). Born at Mitchelstown, Co Cork, and educated at Trinity College, he joined the United Irishmen in 1796 and edited their paper, The Press. *He was arrested and imprisoned in Scotland until 1802. He then joined the French army and was appointed general by Napoleon.*

COUNTDOWN

The army, upon which so much would depend in the event of a rising, was a major source of worry. General Abercromby, appointed to introduce order and discipline, described it as being 'in a state of licentiousness which must render it formidable to everyone except the enemy'. He was disgusted by the actions of the gentry, who, having terrorised the peasantry by their viciousness and lack of sensibility, were now clamouring for government protection. Abercromby soon fell foul of the ruling oligarchy, his emphasis on legality and the humane treatment of civilians being regarded as virtual treason. He was forced to resign and the way was now open for the sectarian cabal, led by John Foster and Lord Clare, to exert influence on the Viceroy, Lord Camden.

In February, Arthur O'Connor was arrested in London, leaving the radical wing of the revolutionaries under the leadership of Lord Edward FitzGerald.

ARREST OF THE LEINSTER DIRECTORY

As the country slid into rebellion, the one group by which the government was well served was its spies. Chief among these were Leonard McNally

Photo 14. John Sheares (1766–98). Educated at Trinity College, he visited France with his brother in 1792 and became an enthusiastic supporter of revolutionary principles. Following the arrest of the principal United Irishmen in March 1798, he became a senior figure in the movement. Captured in May, he was hanged publicly in front of Newgate jail on 14 July.

Photo 15. Henry Sheares (1755–98). Educated at Trinity College, he joined the British army but in the 1790s became converted to the principles of the French Revolution. Arrested with his brother John in May 1798, he was found guilty of high treason and hanged on 14 July.

and Thomas Reynolds. The former was a radical barrister, the latter a rich silk merchant. Reynolds, a relative of Lord Edward FitzGerald, was colonel for County Kildare in the United Irish army and a delegate to its Leinster Directory. In March he tipped off the government that the Leinster Directory was due to meet at the home of one of its members, the Dublin wool merchant, Oliver Bond, on 12 March.

The authorities acted, a party of police surrounded the house and arrested its occupants, ten provincial delegates and two members of the Supreme Executive. Of the senior figures, only Lord Edward remained at large. The government now declared martial law, the army was 'given its head' and searches, floggings and hangings became commonplace. Already, by late 1797, Ulster and parts of North Leinster had been singled out, terrorised and cowed by such methods. The attention of the army now switched to mid-Leinster, and highly organised counties such as Kildare and Carlow were particularly targeted.

The United Irish leaders who were still free set up a new Directory, which included John and Henry Sheares and Samuel Neilson. They still hoped for French aid, but it became increasingly apparent that the rising would have to be soon or not at all.

Photo 16. Militia medals, c. 1798–80. The militia regiments, organised on a county basis, played a major part in the suppression of the rebellion, but gained an infamous reputation for wanton cruelty.

The army had been given 'free quarters' — billeted in the homes of the people — in disturbed districts and this led to the large-scale surrender of arms as the 'pacification measures' began to take effect. Sir John Moore in Cork, General Dundas in Kildare and Sir Charles Asgill in Kilkenny all reported the handing up of pikes and muskets. Wellesley-Pole, the Duke of Wellington's brother, reported drily from Laois, that 'we generally took poultry, pigs, calves, hay and corn from those people but with moderation . . . very few people were twice plundered'. Inhabitants were so terrified that some tried to lay hands on pikes, simply so that they could surrender them and 'clear their names'. Army brutality not only terrified but obviously alienated its victims and it was this mixture of terror and anger, coupled with the unbridled viciousness of the authorities, which was to play a major part in igniting the rebellion.

In south Kildare, the army embarked on a policy of wholesale house-burning and plundered the Quaker village of Ballitore. It was in Kildare, too, that the infamous 'triangle' first appeared. Named for its shape, it was a simple wooden frame to which victims were tied before being flogged and tortured. It was soon in widespread use, as the army and its yeomanry auxiliaries proceeded to flog the country into submission. Athy was singled out for particular attention, while, in the northern part of the county, homes of suspected United Irish supporters were burned in Maynooth, Celbridge and Kilcock. The army next turned its attention to Wicklow, inflicting punishment indiscriminately on guilty and innocent alike.

By now the republican leaders were in a desperate dilemma. A rising without French aid had little chance of success, but if they did not move quickly the organisation would be destroyed anyway. The leaders who were still at large, including FitzGerald, the Sheares brothers and John Lawless, decided to act. As they finalised their plans, however, they were betrayed to the authorities by Edward Magan, a member of the Executive, and Captain Armstrong, a government spy. FitzGerald was arrested after a fierce struggle, during which he was wounded and a member of the arresting party killed. Neilson and the Sheares brothers were also captured and, with them, a proclamation declaring independence and encouraging the people to rise up against their oppressors.

The yeomanry were now let loose on Dublin, with the usual results — house-burnings, floggings and shootings. A considerable quantity of arms was found and the Viceroy began to believe that,

Photo 18. Government proclamation, 1798, demanding the surrender of the United Irishmen and the handing up of their arms.

Photo 19. Captain Swayne pitchcapping prisoners at Prosperous, Co Kildare. Pitchcapping involved the placing of a canvas cap, soaked in pitch or tar, on the head of the victim and setting it on fire. It was a method of torture widely used by the government forces.

with the capital 'cleansed', the threat was over. Despite the arrests, however, the word had spread that 23 May was to be the date for the long-awaited rebellion. When the date arrived, it erupted first and fiercest in Kildare, the county which had suffered most from the army's 'pacification' measures.

THE RISING IN KILDARE

In spite of and partly because of the activities of the military, Kildare still had a considerable body of committed revolutionaries. Led by figures such as Michael Reynolds of Johnstown, William Aylmer of Painstown, Hugh Ware of Maynooth and Dr John Esmonde of Sallins, many of them were landowners who had received military training in the yeomanry. They also possessed the element of surprise. General Dundas, the local army commander, had just declared that 'the County of Kildare will, for a long time, enjoy profound peace and quiet'. He was very wrong.

Pl 1. (Facing page) Henry Grattan (1746–1820). A brilliant orator and respected politician, he gave his name to 'Grattan's Parliament' and to an entire era.

On the night of 23 May, the rebels attacked and wiped out the garrison of Prosperous. The garrison commander, Captain Swayne, was a particularly hated figure whose 'speciality', when interrogating prisoners, was to hang his victims from a beam, with one foot resting on a spike, in order to 'loosen their tongues'. Swayne was shot and his body burned in a barrel of tar. A number of attacks were launched on the nearby village of Clane, forcing the garrison to retreat to Naas. Over one thousand poorly-armed men, led by Michael Reynolds, a local farmer, then launched a fierce attack on the strongly fortified county town. After an hour of desperate fighting, they were finally

cont. p 33

"UNITED IRELAND."

Supplement Gratis with

Saturday, April 17th, 1886.

Henry Grattan

Pl 2. George Washington (1732–99). The American War of Independence had a major influence on Irish political life, encouraging the growth of the Volunteers and fuelling demands for free trade and legislative freedom.

Pl 3. James Napper Tandy (1740–1803). A Dublin ironmonger prominent in the Volunteer movement, Tandy joined the United Irishmen on its foundation and was forced to flee to France in 1793. Landed briefly in Donegal with French forces in 1798. Captured in Hamburg and handed over to the British, he was sentenced to death but released at the request of Napoleon in 1802. He died in Bordeaux in 1803.

Pl 4. Volunteer jug, with slogan 'A Free Trade for Ireland', c. 1780.

Pl 5. Volunteer jug, inscribed 'Success to the Irish Volunteers'. Public support for the aims of the Volunteers was reflected in the slogans and toasts which were a notable feature on contemporary glass, ceramics, textiles and other media.

Pl 6. Earl Fitzwilliam, Viceroy 1795–96. A political liberal, Fitzwilliam immediately fell foul of the reactionary clique which controlled the Irish Government and was soon withdrawn. His removal ushered in the countdown to rebellion.

Pl 7. Lord Edward FitzGerald (1763–98). Born at Carton, Co Kildare, he led an adventurous life as a soldier in the British army and as an explorer in Canada. Greatly influenced by the French Revolution, he returned to Ireland and became a leader of the United Irishmen. Arrested in May 1798, he died of wounds received during his capture.

*Pl 8. On 19 May
1798 Lord Edward
FitzGerald was
arrested by a party
of police under
Major Sirr, but
only after a fierce
struggle during
which one of his
captors was killed
and he himself
wounded.*

Pl 9. The capture
of Lord Edward
FitzGerald. One of
the few United
Irish leaders with
military experience,
his death was a
major blow to the
organisation.

Pl 10. Keys of
Lord Edward
FitzGerald's cell in
Newgate jail,
Dublin. Wounded
in a fierce struggle
during his capture,
he died of his
wounds in
Newgate on 4 June
1798.

Pl 11. Napoleon Bonaparte (1769–1821). Napoleon's decision to conquer Egypt distracted French attention from Ireland at a crucial time and made it more difficult for the United Irishmen to secure substantial aid.

Pl 12. Contemporary illustration of the battle of Tara, 26 May 1798. The United Irish forces, although far superior in numbers, were poorly organised and totally inexperienced. Their defeat signalled the end of the rebellion in Meath.

Pl 13. An insurgent leader at Wexford. From a contemporary illustration.

*Pl 14. Battle of New Ross, 5 June 1798.
The fiercest and bloodiest battle of the
rebellion, it was followed by an orgy of
shooting and looting by the victors that
shocked even their own commanders. The
failure of the insurgents to break out of
Wexford marked a turning point in the
rebellion.*

*Pl 15. Battle of Arklow, 9 June 1798. The
defeat of the United Irishmen put an end
to their advance northwards and forced
them back into Wexford.*

Pl 16. Commemorative wall plaque depicting the death of Fr Michael Murphy at the battle of Arklow. The death of Fr Murphy was a severe blow to the morale of the insurgent forces.

Pl 17. Battle of Vinegar Hill, 21 June 1798. The insurgents, although strong in numbers, were poorly armed and took a fierce pounding from General Lake's artillery on the exposed hillside before they were defeated and scattered.

Pl 18. Membership card, 1798 commemoration society. The illustration shows Michael Dwyer fighting his way out of a burning house in Co Wicklow and is based on the story of one of his many escapes from the military, who sought for years to capture him.

ESCAPE OF MICHAEL DWYER

ⅾⅇⅰⅿⅰnⅰᵹⅽⅇⱥⱤ ᵹuⱤ ⰱⱥⰱⰱ ⅾⅇ Ć
Ćⅰⰱⰱⅇ Ⰿⱥnnⱦⱥⅰn _____

Ⅽuⰱⰱnⅰᵹⅰ _____
Ćⅰⰱⰱⅇ

HOUSE IN GLEN IMAAL, 1798

ann Čuimneačáin 1798 ıʒ Co

ar 1798
ntáin

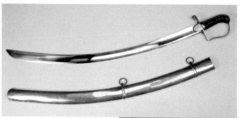

Pl 19. *Presentation sword, battle of Ballinamuck.
Given the size of the British army, the outcome of the
battle was inevitable. The French prisoners were
transported to Dublin while their Irish allies were cut
down on the spot, or hanged in the neighbouring
towns, some being forced to draw lots for the hangman.*

Pl 20. *Medal awarded to
Limerick Militia, battle of
Collooney, 1798. They were
defeated by General Humbert, but
the engagement dissuaded him
from attacking Sligo.*

Pl 21. *Blunderbuss
owned by Michael
Dwyer. It was handed
over by him when he
finally surrendered in
December 1803.*

Pl 22. *Pocketbook
of Theobald Wolfe
Tone. Signed in
prison, November
1798.*

Pl 23. *(Facing page)
Wolfe Tone in the
uniform of a French
adjutant-general, 1797
(from a watercolour by F
Glenn Thompson).*

Pl 24. Michael Dwyer (1771–1826). Dwyer was one of the bravest and most determined of the guerrilla leaders who continued to fight on after 1798. He held out against British forces in Wicklow until 1803. Transported to Australia, he later became High Constable of Sydney.

Pl 25. Robert Emmet (1778–1803). A younger brother of Thomas Addis Emmet, he went to Europe following the collapse of the rebellion. He returned in 1802 to organise another uprising, but the attempt, in July 1803, failed completely. Captured and sentenced to death, he was hanged in Dublin on 20 September 1803.

Pl 26. Commemorative badges, 1898. The hundredth anniversary commemorations provided a major focus for nationalist sentiment and rejuvenated the republican movement.

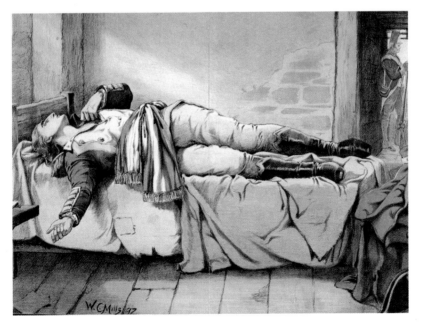

Pl 27. The death of Wolfe Tone. Attempting to commit suicide, Tone succeeded only in cutting his windpipe, prompting his wry observation, 'I fear I am but a bad anatomist.' A government official was so annoyed at not being able to hang him that he commented, 'I would have sewn up his neck and finished the business.'

Pl 28. Death mask of Robert Emmet. Emmet's speech from the dock, and the brave manner in which he met his death, gained him a lasting place in Irish history.

cont. from p 16

driven back, their raw courage no match
for the artillery of the military. They left
three hundred of their number dead on
the streets of the town.

The rebellion now moved south. The
rebels, armed largely with pikes, routed the
army at Old Kilcullen but were in turn
routed and massacred at nearby Kilcullen
Bridge. Their ferocity and courage,
however, panicked General Dundas, who withdrew his troops to Naas
and Athy. The rebels promptly took Newbridge and Kildare and
attacked Monasterevan. From Kildare, fighting erupted in all directions.
To the south, the rebels attacked Carlow and Hacketstown on 25 May
but were beaten off, with huge losses. To the west, Rathangan was
captured and armed columns pushed into Laois and Offaly. In the
north, Kilcock, Leixlip and Lucan were attacked and groups of Kildare-
men marched into Meath, linking up with local United Irish forces at
Dunboyne. To the south-east the rebellion spread into Wicklow and
Wexford, less through United Irish leadership than fear, rumour and
the news from Kildare.

*Photo 20. A
Wexford pikeman.
From a
contemporary
illustration.*

Most Catholics had by this stage been forced out of, or had resigned
from, the yeomanry — some to join the rebellion — so that it was
almost exclusively Protestant, controlled by the most anti-Catholic element
of the loyalist community. To these were added groups of freelancers,
such as the Black Mob, a gang led by the notorious Hunter Gowan in
Wexford, which gained a fearsome reputation for casual violence.

Atrocities were committed on
both sides, but the excesses of the
insurgents, with a few horrific
exceptions, did not compare to
the calculated barbarities of some
of the yeomanry and militia
corps.

*Photo 21.
Government
proclamation,
Dublin, 4 June
1798. Inhabitants
were ordered to
place lights in
their windows
should there be any
alarm. Those
failing to do so
were threatened
with severe
punishment. The
city was in a state
of great tension,
particularly as
news of the
Wexford rebellion
filtered through.*

Photo 22. Oath issued by the United Irishmen in Wexford, June 1798. The taker of the oath swore that he would endeavour 'to form a Brotherhood of affection among Irishmen of every religious persuasion'.

WAR IN WEXFORD

The rebellion now broke out in Wexford, fanned by army searches, stories of atrocities in Wicklow and rumours that Catholics were about to be massacred by the Orangemen. The atrocity stories were all too true. At Dunlavin, on 24 May, thirty-four prisoners, including twenty-eight yeomen suspected of being United Irish sympathisers, were lined up on the fair-green and shot. Further south at Carnew, the following day, a similar number of prisoners were taken out and slaughtered in the local ball-alley.

The Catholic peasantry of north Wexford, terrified by the stories reaching them from Wicklow and angered by the daily flogging and house-burning, rose in rebellion. They were led by two local Catholic priests, Fr John Murphy and Fr Michael Murphy. Armed largely with scythes, pitchforks and pikes, they routed a military column at Oulart on 26 May and almost immediately took the towns of Ferns and Gorey. Enniscorthy was threatened and the stage was set for the bloodiest phase of the rebellion.

COLLAPSE OF THE RISING IN NORTH LEINSTER

On the very day that the rebellion erupted in Wexford, it was beginning to collapse further north. The attempt to encircle Dublin had failed, following minor skirmishes around Tallaght and Rathcoole in the south and Santry in the north. In Meath, a poorly armed force of United Irishmen was routed at the battle of Tara on 26 May, leaving an estimated three hundred and fifty dead on the historic hill.

The military action now focused back on Kildare, where many of the rebels, short of arms and supplies, favoured negotiation with the government. One group, encamped near Kilcullen, agreed terms with General Dundas and dispersed. A second contingent, at Gibbet Rath on the Curragh, about to do likewise, were surrendering their arms to the same commander when they were attacked by other government forces under General Duff. An estimated four hundred largely unarmed rebels were massacred before Duff called off his troops. Ballitore was retaken and gutted by government forces from Carlow. Rathangan was the scene of fierce fighting before also being retaken. The defeated rebels retreated north to join the last substantial Kildare army still holding out under William Aylmer at Timahoe.

As the rebellion faltered in Kildare, it grew fiercer in Wexford. Enniscorthy was taken on 28 May and the defeated yeomanry retreated south, shooting civilians as they went. Wexford itself was now surrounded. A relief column got to within a few miles of the town before being ambushed and wiped out by an army of Wexford pikemen at the battle of Three Rocks. The Wexford garrison panicked and abandoned the town, shooting and burning as they went. The rebels promptly occupied the town on 30 May. Loyalists were hunted down and lodged in the overcrowded jail, but, in general, according to the historian Lecky, the rebels 'committed far less outrages than might reasonably have been expected'. A government counter-attack was repulsed. The entire county, with the exception of New Ross, was now in the hands of the rebels.

THE REBELLION IN ULSTER

Early in June the long-awaited rising in Ulster broke out. Originally the strongest United Irish base, the north had borne the full brunt of General Lake's 'pacification' measures the previous year. The movement had also been weakened by sectarian tensions, which were never far from the surface in Ulster and which the government was only too willing to exploit. On 6 June, however, the United Irishmen of Antrim, led by Henry Joy McCracken and Samuel Orr, rose in rebellion. Many of the Defenders, the Catholic agrarian society which was partly integrated into the United Irish movement, stayed aloof, so that it became a largely Presbyterian army. The towns of Randalstown and Ballymena were captured, but the assault on Antrim town failed.

The garrison was reinforced just as McCracken's force attacked and after fierce fighting his army was routed, leaving three hundred dead on the streets. The government troops celebrated their victory in the

Photo 23. Henry Joy McCracken (1767–98). A native of Belfast, he was a founder member of the United Irishmen. Commanded the insurgents at the battle of Antrim, 7 June 1798. Escaped and hid for some time in the Slemish mountains. Captured and condemned to death, he was hanged in Belfast on 17 July 1798.

NOTICE.

WHEREAS a great many of the Leaders and Principal Agitators in the Rebellion, have secreted themselves in the County of Down, and go through the Country during the Night to persuade and force the People to rise again in Arms; I hereby offer a Reward of FIFTY GUINEAS for the Apprehension of each of the following Persons. I also warn the Inhabitants of the County in general, that if any of them are convicted of harbouring one or more of those Persons, or knowing where they are, do not give immediate Notice thereof, to the Officer Commanding at the nearest Post, they will suffer as capital Offenders, and their Property be destroyed. Should any Person be weak or wicked enough to join those desperate Outlaws, either by Force or from Inclination, he cannot expect Mercy; and I therefore conjure every one to give immediate Information against such Persons as may go through the Country for the Purposes above-mentioned, and also to do all in their Power to take them up.

If the People do not attend to this Warning, they will have none but themselves to blame for the Distresses brought on their Families.

G. NUGENT, Major-General,

Belfast, July 18, 1798.   Commanding Northern District.

John Beatty, of Knockbracken.   — Davidson, a Col. near Ballynahinch.
Andrew Bryson, of Newtownards.   Joseph Thompson, of Ballyrush.
Richard Frazer, of Ravarra.   William Minals, of Lisloonan.
James Ham Leon, of Moneyrea.   The Rev. Mr. Adair, near Comber.
Nevin Kearns, of Magherascouse.   Doctor Jackson, of Newtownards.
Hugh Laughlin, of Ballygraffin.   Doctor Shields, of or near Comber.
John M'Cardlin, of Cardymoor.   — M'Cance, of or near Ballynahinch
The Rev Js. Townsend, of Greyabby.   Thomas Mathews, near Saintfield.
David Thompson, of Saintfield.   — Sibbet, sen. } of Killinchy.
James Wightman, of Bryanthurn.   — Torney, }
Thomas Rainey,   Revd. James Hull.
The Rev. Mr. Warwick, of Kircubbin.

Photo 24. Reward of fifty guineas for the capture of insurgents in Co Down, July 1798. The inhabitants were warned that anyone harbouring a fugitive, or failing to provide information to the authorities, would 'suffer as capital offenders and their property be destroyed'.

usual manner. Prisoners and suspects were rounded up, shot and dumped in a local sandpit. An amnesty was then offered, most of the fugitives accepted and the rebellion fizzled out — just as it erupted in neighbouring County Down.

Photo 25. The battle of Vinegar Hill, from an illustration by George Cruikshanke. The artist, who was strongly pro-loyalist, depicted the insurgents in the most unflattering manner possible.

Here the organisation had been riddled with spies and many of the leaders had been arrested before the rebellion broke out. On 9 June, however, a force of about seven thousand gathered at Saintfield in the middle of the county, under Henry Monroe, a Lisburn draper. Ballynahinch and Newtownards were captured, but the rebel army was poorly organised and dogged by distrust and friction between Presbyterians and Catholics. It was soon under attack from north and south. Saintfield was abandoned by the rebels and burned by the advancing army, which then moved on to attack the main rebel position at Ballynahinch on 13 June. There followed a bloody engagement in the streets of the town, during which the United Irish pikemen launched several attacks on their enemies' artillery but were 'blown from the mouth of the cannon like chaff'. They were forced to retreat and the fleeing survivors were mowed down by government cavalry. Among the casualties was Betsy Gray, a young United Irish volunteer who had fought alongside her male companions and rallied the pikemen on several occasions during the battle. Monroe was hanged outside his own door and, according to some reports, in front of his wife and sisters. The Antrim commander, McCracken, was hanged in Belfast. Several other 'salutary' executions were carried out, followed by a general amnesty. The Ulster rebellion was over.

THE TURNING OF THE TIDE

In Wexford, the bloodiest battle of the entire rebellion was fought at New Ross on 5 June. Under the rather ineffectual leadership of Bagenal Harvey, a Protestant landlord and senior United Irishman, the rebels launched a fierce assault on the strategic town. They breached the defences but were forced back, rallied a second time to take the town but were finally dislodged in a counter-attack. Armed with pikes, scythes and pitchforks, they continued their desperate attempts to capture the artillery of the enemy before being driven back, with great slaughter. The loyalist forces, a motley collection of yeomanry, militia and British regulars, then went on an orgy of looting that lasted for several days,

*Photo 26. John
Henry Colclough, a
leader of the
United Irishmen in
Wexford. Following
the collapse of the
rebellion, he fled to
the Saltee Islands
with his wife and
Bagenal Harvey,
but they were
discovered and
captured. Both
men were hanged
and beheaded.*

hanging and shooting suspected rebels out of hand.

The total death toll for the battle and its aftermath was estimated at over three thousand. A few miles away at Scullabogue, an angry mob, incensed by the news filtering through from New Ross, retaliated by massacring over one hundred loyalist prisoners held in a makeshift jail. Many of them, including some women and children, were burned alive. Bagenal Harvey, discouraged by New Ross and sickened by the Scullabogue atrocity, resigned command of the rebel army to Fr Philip Roche.

A few days after New Ross, the northern wing of the Wexford army, aided by a large contingent of Wicklow-men, attacked Arklow, the gateway to Wicklow and Dublin. Led by Fr Michael Murphy, a Catholic priest, and Anthony Perry, a Protestant landowner, they made a fierce

*Photo 27. The
capture of Bagenal
Harvey and John
Henry Colclough.
From an
illustration by
George
Cruikshanke.*

but poorly co-ordinated attack on the town, carrying a green flag on which were the words 'Liberty or Death'. As at Naas, New Ross and Ballynahinch, however, courage was insufficient against artillery and cavalry. They were defeated, with heavy losses. Fr Michael Murphy was killed in a desperate charge on the enemy cannon.

Large numbers of British troops were now arriving in the country and a major assault on Wexford got under way. In the meantime, Wexford town was ruled by a Committee of Public Safety, headed by a military governor, Matthew Keogh. The Committee organised the distribution of food, set up a system of policing and curbed looting. As the atrocities of the government forces, especially after New Ross, became known, there was mounting anger among the refugees who filled the town. A mob attacked the jail, which held loyalist prisoners. Despite the efforts of the United Irish leadership and several Catholic priests, the prisoners were taken out and murdered — almost one hundred in all.

On 21 June the main insurgent camp in north Wexford, at Vinegar Hill, was attacked by General Lake, his army augmented by the two resources that the rebels lacked — artillery and cavalry. Following a bloody encounter, the pikemen were defeated, but many of them escaped through what became known as 'Needham's Gap', named after the British general who had failed to complete their encirclement. Lake's victory was followed by wholesale death and destruction around Enniscorthy. The insurgents' field hospital was set on fire, with the wounded still inside, and fugitives were shot out of hand. Meanwhile, a second British army force defeated a United Irish force at Foulksmills on 20 June and headed for Wexford town.

Organised resistance collapsed, but many of the defenders escaped into Carlow and Wicklow. When Fr Philip Roche, leader of the dwindling United Irish army, rode into Wexford to negotiate surrender, he was beaten senseless, court-martialled and hanged.

Photo 28. Skirmish between yeomanry and insurgents at Killoughrim Wood, near Enniscorthy, 1804. Guerrilla warfare continued sporadically in Wexford and Wicklow long after the rebellion had been suppressed.

Bagenal Harvey and another United Irish leader, Henry Colclough, fled to the Saltee Islands but were captured and suffered the same fate, as did Matthew Keogh, governor of the town during its brief independence. Their heads were placed on spikes at the courthouse. The 'Republic of Wexford' was at an end.

The viciousness which characterised General Lake's mopping up operations hardened the resolve of the insurgents still in the field. One group, under Fr John Murphy, fought their way into Carlow, Kilkenny and Laois, in a vain attempt to rally support, but were forced back into Wexford. A second army, under Anthony Perry and Edward FitzGerald, marched into Kildare to link up with forces still holding out there. On 10 July they made contact with the Kildare-men, under William Aylmer, at Timahoe. Aylmer's men had been heavily defeated at Ovidstown, near Kilcock, on 19 June, after earlier successes at Kilcock and Maynooth. The recapture of Prosperous by loyalist forces made their situation impossible and they were on the point of surrender when the Wexford-men arrived.

Aylmer decided to remain at Timahoe, but most of the Wexford-men, under Anthony Perry and Edward FitzGerald, with some Wicklow and Kildare contingents, kept moving. They marched into Meath, crossed the Boyne and fought their way through the encircling enemy at the battle of Knightstown. They pushed as far as the Louth border, desperately seeking other United armies that no longer existed. Hungry, tired and dependent on pikes against well-armed cavalry, the ragged army dwindled and was finally routed and dispersed at Ballyboughal in north Dublin. FitzGerald struggled back to Timahoe and, along with Aylmer, surrendered to Lord Cornwallis. The indomitable Perry and another leader, Fr Kearns, were captured by the yeomanry and hanged in Edenderry.

Their desperate march had taken them through six counties. Following the collapse of the rebellion, the victorious loyalists embarked on a campaign of terror in an effort to cow the country and track down the remnants of the United Irish leadership. In Carlow, more than one hundred unfortunates, many of them unassociated with the insurrection, were flogged by the garrison, Fourteen of them were hanged. In Wexford, the military declared 'open season' on the inhabitants and it was claimed that over two hundred people were murdered between Enniscorthy and the Carlow border. In Mountmellick, at least a dozen men were hanged, while the deranged High Sheriff of Tipperary, Judkin Fitzgerald, flogged his way through the county, unconcerned by questions of guilt or innocence. There were over thirty 'official' hangings in Antrim and Down, more than a dozen in the town of Newtownards alone. The prisons filled up and the overflow was accommodated on convict ships while the authorities decided their fate. By August the country was quiet, apart from sporadic guerrilla attacks, especially in Wicklow and Wexford.

The action now moved from the battlefield to the courtroom. There were over eighty 'State prisoners' in various Dublin jails, most of them imprisoned during the crackdown which preceded the rebellion. Evidence against many of them was flimsy, but informers provided sufficient information to send some to the gallows. The Sheares brothers were first to be tried. They were found guilty, hanged and beheaded. They were followed by John McCann and William Byrne, members of the Leinster Directory. At this point, the other leaders offered to make a full admission of their activities, to save their lives and those of their followers. Cornwallis accepted the offer, the executions ceased and the prisoners were dispatched to Fort St George in the Scottish Highlands. They were released and banished in 1802.

THE EXPEDITION OF GENERAL HUMBERT

The Irish exiles in Paris, including Wolfe Tone, Samuel Orr, Edward Lewins and Napper Tandy, had spent the spring and summer seeking French aid, but Napoleon was intent on the more exotic task of conquering Egypt. When the French were finally persuaded to act, the

Photo 30.
Government
communiqué of 29
August 1798,
carrying news of
the French victory
at Castlebar.

Photo 31.
Proclamation
issued by the
French at Killala,
August 1798. The
stirring manifesto
proclaimed the
birth of an Irish
republic, but the
limited nature of
the French aid
ensured that its
existence was
shortlived.

principal element of the invasion army, four thousand men under General Hardy, failed to break the British blockade of Brest. Another proposed force did not materialise.

One group, a little army of eleven hundred men from La Rochelle under General Humbert, succeeded in evading the British and landed at Killala, Co Mayo, on 23 August. Against this little expeditionary force and the handful of Irish exiles who accompanied it, Lord Cornwallis had at his disposal a huge army of British regulars, yeomanry and militia.

Humbert was joined by large numbers of local people, enthusiastic but totally untrained. The yeomanry fled before him and on 25 August he took Ballina. He promptly moved on Castlebar, where a British army was gathering under General Lake, arriving before the town on 27 August after an overnight march. Following a brief engagement, the French charged and their enemies broke and fled in all directions. Some retreated as far as Athlone, sixty miles away, such was the terror inspired by the French. The 'Races of Castlebar', as it became known, boosted the morale of the Franco-Irish army, while General Lake's soldiers, even in retreat, found time to plunder the inhabitants, fanning the rebellion that they were attempting to suppress.

The Viceroy, Lord Cornwallis, now took personal control of the government forces. Aware of the poor calibre of his troops, he moved slowly towards Castlebar.

Humbert, meanwhile, tightened his grip on Mayo and threatened Sligo, the

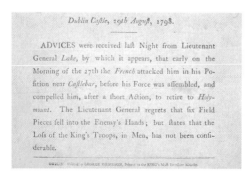

*Photo 32. Bust of
General Joseph
Humbert. A
veteran of several
campaigns,
Humbert was an
energetic
commander whose
little army tied
down vastly
superior British
forces for several
weeks.*

*Photo 33.
Bartholomew
Teeling (1744–98).
The son of a
Lisburn draper, he
joined the United
Irishmen and, in
1796, went to
France to join
Wolfe Tone.
Landed at Killala
in 1798 as aide-
de-camp to
General Humbert.
Captured by the
British after the
battle of
Ballinamuck, he
was sentenced to
death and executed
at Arbour Hill,
Dublin, on 24
September.*

British having abandoned Swinford and Foxford. John Moore, member of a prominent local family, was appointed president of the provisional government of Connacht and a committee was elected to help him govern. Locals who flocked to Humbert's army were organised into battalions and regiments. There was still a sprinkling of Catholic gentry in Mayo and it was from this group that he drew his chief supporters. Colonel John McDonnell organised the raw recruits and Matt Bellew, who had fought in the Austrian and Russian armies, was appointed General. Leitrim and Roscommon remained quiet, however, and Humbert marched towards Sligo, routing a force of yeomanry and militia at Collooney. He decided against attacking Sligo and was about to strike out into Ulster when he heard heartening news from another quarter. Rebellion had broken out in

*Photo 34. The
surrender of
General Humbert
at Ballinamuck, 8
September 1798.*

Photo 35.
Theobald Wolfe
Tone (1763–98) in
French uniform.
From a
contemporary
illustration.

Photo 36. Wolfe
Tone's pocket-book,
inscribed 'TW
Tone Nov 11th
1798'. Tone cut his
own throat the
following day,
when his request to
be executed by
firing squad was
refused.

Longford and Westmeath. He immediately swung round and marched through Leitrim to make contact with the rebels. His march was in vain. By the time he reached the Longford border, his potential allies had been defeated and dispersed.

The United Irishmen had remained strong in Longford and Westmeath, despite the army's terror tactics the previous summer. Encouraged by news of Humbert's successes, they rose on 4 September, gathering in large numbers on the Longford/Westmeath border. The rebellion was similar to that of Wexford, a mixture of agrarian, sectarian and political. The demand that 'every man should have equal riches' became unavoidably sectarian in practice, since most of the agricultural and commercial wealth and all the political power was in the hands of Protestants. It should be emphasised, however, that, as in Wexford and Wicklow, some of the principal insurgent leaders in the midlands were Protestants. Led by one such, Hans Denniston, a prosperous farmer, the Longford army attacked Granard but was routed with huge losses. The Westmeath rebels were attacked by government forces at Wilson's hospital, north of Mullingar. Led by Christopher Barden, a local miller, they charged the enemy cannon 'with an audacity not easily understood' but were driven back and slaughtered. Brave but poorly armed, untrained and lacking experienced leaders, they were no match for the well-armed British regulars and cavalry. A small number of survivors from the Granard fight escaped to the French camp at Cloone, Co Leitrim.

Humbert pushed on into Longford but was finally forced to give battle against vastly superior forces at

Ballinamuck on 8 September. He decided that it was pointless to fight on and surrendered after a brief engagement. His troops were treated as prisoners of war. Their Irish allies, however, were treated as rebels and butchered in their hundreds. Many more were captured and hanged, including their commander, George Blake. Fugitives rounded up during the following days were executed in the surrounding towns of Longford, Granard, Cavan and Carrick-on-Shannon. Wolfe Tone's younger brother, Matthew, and General Humbert's aide-de-camp, Bartholomew Teeling, were taken to Dublin, court-martialled and hanged at Arbour Hill.

The final episode was still to come. Encouraged by Humbert's early successes, the French, too late, had managed to send reinforcements. A body of two hundred and seventy French soldiers, together with

Photo 37. Joseph Holt (1756–1826). A Protestant farmer with no political affiliations, he joined the rebels when his house was burned by the military. His guerrilla tactics pinned down large government forces in Wicklow for months after the collapse of the rebellion. He surrendered and was transported to Botany Bay, Australia.

Photo 38. Michael Dwyer (1771–1826). Dwyer held out in the Wicklow mountains until after the collapse of Emmet's attempted rebellion in 1803.

Photo 39. Robert Emmet addressing the court during his trial, 1803. He concluded his speech with the famous words: 'When my country takes her place among the nations of the earth, then, and not til then, let my epitaph be written.'

some Irish exiles under Napper Tandy, landed at Rutland Island, off the Donegal coast, on 16 September. Discovering that Humbert had already surrendered, they sailed away again. Killala, last bastion of the 'Republic of Connacht', fell on 23 September, a month from the date of Humbert's landing and four months from the date of the original rising in Kildare. Its defenders put up a fierce resistance but were overwhelmed and virtually wiped out. The victorious troops proceeded to pillage the townspeople, loyalists and rebels alike, the Protestant bishop of Killala noting that the militia were 'incomparably superior to the Irish traitors in dexterity of Stealing'. When there was nothing left to shoot or loot, the army marched away.

On 12 October the long-awaited expeditionary force from Brest, over three thousand strong, was intercepted off Tory Island by the British navy and defeated. Among those taken prisoner was Wolfe Tone.

Tone was taken to Dublin and charged with treason. He did not deny the charges, declaring, 'I admit the charges against me in the fullest extent; what I have done I have done and I am prepared to stand the consequences. The great object of my life has been the independence of my country; for that I have sacrificed everything most dear to man.' He explained his actions, finishing as follows: 'I have attempted to establish the independence of my country; I have failed in that attempt. My life is in consequence forfeited and I submit. The court will do their duty and I shall endeavour to do mine.' He was sentenced to death by hanging. When his request to be executed by firing squad was refused, he slashed his throat with

*Photo 41. Capture
of Thomas Russell,
14 August 1803.
Russell's arrest and
execution and the
surrender of
Michael Dwyer put
an end to any
possibility of
another rebellion.*

a razor. He only succeeded in cutting his windpipe, however, and lingered in agony for a week before dying. His enduring place in Irish history is summed up by the historian Thomas Pakenham: 'His shining virtues — vision, humour and self-sacrifice — set alight the imagination of later nationalists. He came to personify the tradition of violent revolution in Ireland and its successful exponents honour him as few men in Irish history are honoured.'

Guerrilla warfare continued into the late autumn, especially in Wexford, Wicklow and Mayo, but on 10 November — the day of Tone's trial — Joseph Holt, the Wicklow guerrilla leader, surrendered, leaving only the intrepid Michael Dwyer still in the field. Arrests continued into the new year. Large numbers of prisoners were transported to the Australian penal colony of Botany Bay. Others were forced into the British

Photo 42. 1798 centenary handkerchief. The hundredth anniversary in 1898 provided a major morale boost for the republican movement, then at a low ebb.

army and navy. Several hundred were sent to serve in the Prussian army and some are said to have ended their days in the German salt mines.

The United Irishmen made one last attempt at rebellion in 1803, but it ended in total failure. The leader, Robert Emmet, younger brother of Thomas Addis Emmet, was hanged and beheaded in Dublin. Thomas Russell was captured and hanged in Downpatrick. Peace of a kind returned, but it was a bitter peace. The old order was restored, but its upholders, like the Habsburgs, had learned nothing and forgotten nothing. The stage was set for another unsettled chapter in Irish history.

BIBLIOGRAPHY

Dickson, Charles. 1944. *The Life of Michael Dwyer.* Dublin.

Dickson, D, Keogh, D and Whelan, K (eds). 1993. *The United Irishmen: Republicanism, Radicalism and Rebellion.* Dublin.

Elliott, Marianne. 1969. *Wolfe Tone, Prophet of Irish Independence.* New Haven and London.

Furlong, Nicholas. 1991. *Fr John Murphy of Boolavogue, 1753–1798.* Dublin.

Gahan, Daniel. 1995. *The People's Rising: Wexford 1798.* Dublin.

Hayes, Richard. 1937. *The Last Invasion of Ireland.* Dublin.

Lecky, William. 1913. *A History of Ireland in the Eighteenth Century.* Vol 4. London.

MacSuibhne, Peadar. 1974. *'98 in Carlow.* Carlow.

MacSuibhne, Peadar. 1978. *Kildare in '98.* Naas.

Madden, R R. 1842. *The United Irishmen, Their Lives and Times.* Vols I and II. London.

Pakenham, Thomas. 1969. *The Year of Liberty.* London.

Stewart, A T Q. 1995. *The Summer Soldiers: The 1798 Rebellion in Antrim and Down.* Belfast.